SPORTS' GRE...

BASEBALL'S
G.O.A.T.

BABE RUTH, MIKE TROUT, AND MORE

JON M. FISHMAN

Lerner Publications ◆ Minneapolis

Copyright © 2020 by Lerner Publishing Group, Inc.

All rights reserved. International copyright secured. No part of this book may be reproduced, stored in a retrieval system, or transmitted in any form or by any means—electronic, mechanical, photocopying, recording, or otherwise—without the prior written permission of Lerner Publishing Group, Inc., except for the inclusion of brief quotations in an acknowledged review.

Lerner Publications Company
A division of Lerner Publishing Group, Inc.
241 First Avenue North
Minneapolis, MN 55401 USA

For reading levels and more information, look up this title at www.lernerbooks.com.

Main body text set in Aptifer Sans LT Pro.
Typeface provided by Linotype AG.

Library of Congress Cataloging-in-Publication Data

The Cataloging-in-Publication Data for *Baseball's G.O.A.T.: Babe Ruth, Mike Trout, and More* is on file at the Library of Congress.
ISBN 978-1-5415-5598-3 (lib. bdg.)
ISBN 978-1-5415-7441-0 (pbk.)
ISBN 978-1-5415-5632-4 (eb pdf)

Manufactured in the United States of America
1-46054-43470-1/28/2019

CONTENTS

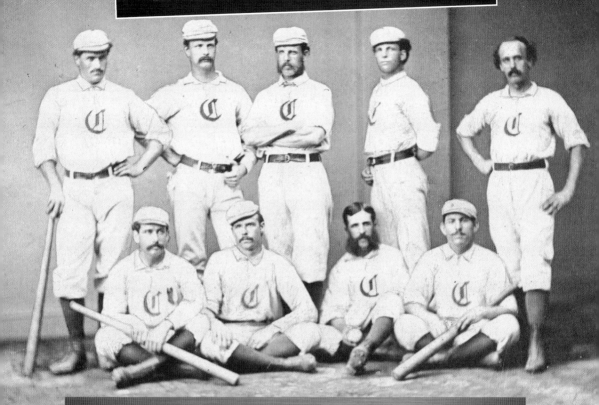

The 1869 Cincinnati Red Stockings were the first all-pro baseball team. They won all 57 games they played.

FIRST PITCH!

Major League Baseball (MLB) has great players at every position. With so many fantastic players, choosing the best is a tall task. When you think about the greatest of all time (G.O.A.T.) in baseball, the job gets even harder.

FACTS AT A GLANCE

BARRY BONDS was a legendary slugger. But he also had a great eye at the plate. His 2,558 walks are the most in MLB history.

TY COBB held 43 MLB all-time records when he retired from the game in 1928.

HANK AARON hit at least 30 home runs in a season 15 times. With 715 home runs, he held the career record for more than 30 years.

SATCHEL PAIGE was voted to play in two All-Star Games despite not joining MLB until he was 41. At the age of 59, he returned to MLB and pitched three scoreless innings.

The first baseball games were played about 175 years ago. In 1869, the Cincinnati Red Stockings became the first pro team. The sport was similar to the modern game. But many MLB rules were different in the 1800s. Then pitchers had to throw underhand and walks counted as hits. MLB didn't even keep accurate stats of players and games.

That changed at the beginning of the 1900s. MLB officials consider 1900 the start of baseball's modern era. Most of the rules were set by then. MLB started to keep careful track

Yet the sport has changed a lot since the dawn of the modern era. Back then, pitchers threw more innings each season. That allowed them to rack up amazing stats that may never be matched. Modern stars are bigger and stronger than ever. They stay fit all year with healthful food and training programs that stars of the past never had.

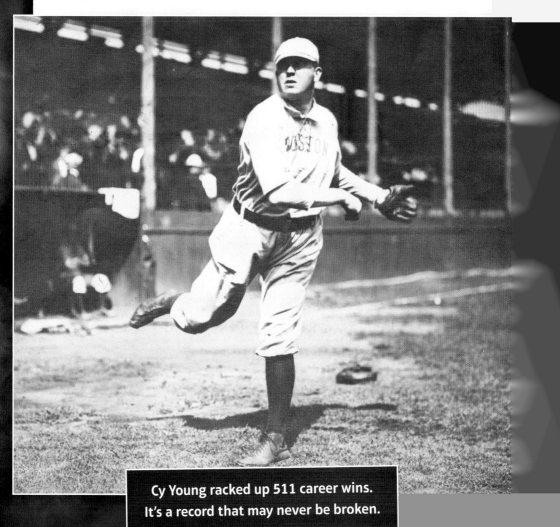

Cy Young racked up 511 career wins.
It's a record that may never be broken.

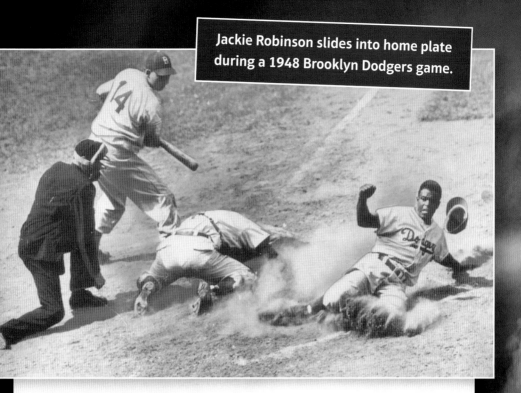

Jackie Robinson slides into home plate during a 1948 Brooklyn Dodgers game.

In 1947, Jackie Robinson joined the Brooklyn Dodgers. He was the modern era's first African American player. For more than 50 years, African Americans and other people of color had been banned from MLB. Some say MLB stats from before 1947 aren't valid because the league excluded many of the world's best players.

Baseball's history gives fans a lot to consider. As you read about the players in this book, you'll form your own opinions about them. You might wonder why some players aren't included. Maybe you will disagree with the order of the players. Opinions about baseball can be as diverse as the players who make the sport great.

#10

MIKE TROUT

Most of baseball's all-time greats enjoyed long careers. They collected hits, wins, and other stats over many years. Mike Trout is just getting started, but he's already one of the greatest of all time. He won the Rookie of the Year Award with the Los Angeles Angels after the 2012 season. Since then, he's gotten even better.

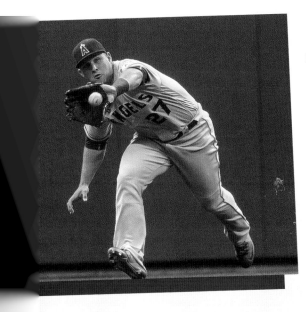

Trout plays center field. With so much of the field to cover, it's one of the most demanding positions in baseball. He races around the outfield to track down balls. He dives to make catches and leaps above the outfield wall to prevent home runs. But Trout is best known for his batting skills. He has hit at least 27 home runs in each full season he's played. Because of his high career batting average and his ability to draw walks, he's often on base. And when he gets on base, his blinding speed helps him score.

MIKE TROUT STATS

- He was voted to play in seven All-Star Games.

- He won the All-Star Game Most Valuable Player (MVP) Award in 2014 and 2015.

- He won the Silver Slugger award five times.

- He led MLB in runs scored in three of his first five full seasons.

- He won the American League (AL) MVP Award in

STAN MUSIAL

From Rogers Hornsby to Albert Pujols, the St. Louis Cardinals have had countless great players. None was better than Stan Musial. He started his career in 1938 as a pitcher. Then a shoulder injury forced him to switch to the outfield. The injury turned out to be a good thing for

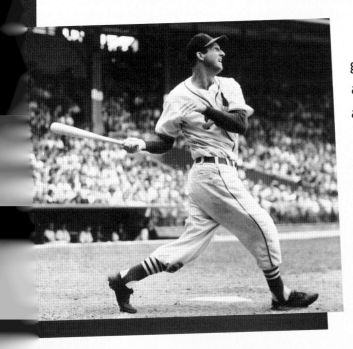

He didn't look like a great hitter. Musial often appeared off-balance at home plate. But his results as a batter were special. Musial led the Cardinals to World Series titles in 1942 and 1944. In 1945, he joined the US Navy during World War II (1939–1945). He was back on the baseball field in 1946 to help the Cardinals win their third World Series in five seasons. When he retired in 1963, his 3,630 hits were the most in National League (NL) history.

STAN MUSIAL STATS

- He was voted to play in 24 All-Star Games.

- He led the NL in batting average seven times.

- He led the NL in hits six times.

- He led the NL in runs scored five times.

- He won the NL MVP Award three times.

ROGER CLEMENS

Few pitchers have ever ruled the game as completely as Roger Clemens did. His nickname was the Rocket for the shocking speed of his fastballs. The blazing pitch helped him win nine games as a rookie with the Boston Red Sox in 1984. Two years later, he won the AL Cy Young Award. The prize is given each year to the best pitcher in each

league. Clemens won the award seven times in his career, two more than any other player. His 4,672 career strikeouts are the third most in MLB history.

Clemens is one of the most debated players in baseball. His stats prove that he deserves a place of honor with the greatest of all time.

But some people have said he used drugs called steroids to make him stronger. That's one reason that even though he retired in 2007, Clemens is not a member of the Baseball Hall of Fame.

ROGER CLEMENS STATS

▶ He was voted to play in 11 All-Star Games.

▶ He led the AL in wins four times.

▶ He won the AL MVP Award in 1986.

▶ He won the AL pitching Triple Crown in 1997 and 1998.

▶ He led his league in earned run average (ERA) seven times.

SATCHEL PAIGE

People of color were banned from MLB before 1947. But they still played pro baseball. The Negro Leagues were pro leagues that thrived early in the 1900s. The teams traveled around the country and featured some of the world's best baseball talent. Perhaps the best of them was pitcher Satchel Paige.

The Negro Leagues often didn't record stats, so many of Paige's feats were kept alive in stories. He pitched hundreds of games each year for different teams. His high leg kick distracted batters before the ball came whizzing past them. In the middle of the 1948 season, Paige got his first MLB job. He was 41 years old when he joined the Cleveland Indians. Paige had a 6–1 record and helped the Indians win the World Series. At the age of 59, he returned to MLB and pitched three scoreless innings for the Kansas City Athletics.

SATCHEL PAIGE STATS

- He was voted to play in two All-Star Games despite not joining MLB until he was 41.

- He was the oldest player in the AL for five seasons.

- He played 40 seasons of pro baseball.

- He was the first African American pitcher to play in the World Series.

- He was the first player who spent most of his career in the Negro Leagues to join the Baseball Hall of Fame.

HANK AARON

Hank Aaron followed in the footsteps of Jackie Robinson and Satchel Paige. Aaron began his career as a teenager in the Negro Leagues. In April 1954, he joined the NL's Milwaukee Braves. He hit his first MLB home run 10 days later. The blast marked the start of one of the most powerful careers in baseball history.

It was almost impossible for a pitcher to throw a fastball past Aaron. His strong hands and wrists gave him a lightning-quick swing. He used it to launch ball after ball out of the park for home runs. In 23 MLB seasons, Aaron racked up some amazing stats. His 2,297 runs batted in (RBIs) are the most ever. On April 8, 1974, Aaron sent a ball soaring over the outfield fence—his 715th home run and the most home runs by a player in baseball history. Aaron held the career home run record for more than 30 years.

HANK AARON STATS

- He was voted to 25 All-Star Games.
- In 1957, he won the NL MVP Award and helped the Braves win the World Series.
- He led the NL in home runs four times.
- He led the NL in runs scored three times.
- He hit at least 30 home runs in a season 15 times.

#5

TED WILLIAMS

Ted Williams wanted to be the best hitter of all time. Some say he reached that goal. Williams focused so much on hitting that he didn't spend much time practicing his outfield defense. But what he lacked in the field, he made up for at home plate.

No batter could track a ball out of the pitcher's hand better than Williams. He knew exactly where the strike zone was and where the ball was going. If it wasn't a good pitch to hit, Williams didn't swing at it. It showed in his stats. His .344 career batting average is tied for seventh all time. His career on-base percentage of .481 is the best ever. He's one of just seven players in the modern era to hit .400 or better in a season. And he did it all despite missing almost five seasons to serve in the US military during wartime.

TED WILLIAMS STATS

- He was voted to play in 19 All-Star Games.
- He led the AL in batting average six times.
- He won the AL MVP Award in 1946 and 1949.
- He won the AL batting Triple Crown in 1942 and 1947.
- He led the AL in runs scored six times.

#4

TY COBB

Ty Cobb was tough. He played baseball as if he were angry and had few friends on the field. Even his own teammates were wary of Cobb's fiery temper. Yet he also played with the passion and skill that made him a legend.

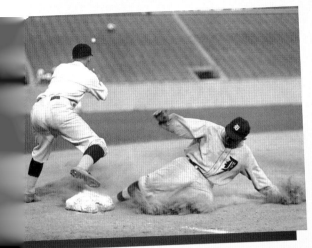

Cobb's career began with the Detroit Tigers in 1905. He spent 22 seasons with the Tigers before finishing his career with the Philadelphia Athletics. Cobb built a reputation as one of the game's greats. He could do it all. He hit for average and power. He stole 897 bases in his career, the fourth most ever. His usual position was in the outfield. He also played in the infield and even pitched. Cobb wasn't stronger or faster than other players. But he was smart and no one worked harder. He retired from pro baseball in 1928. When he left the game, he held 43 MLB all-time records.

TY COBB STATS

- He led the AL in runs scored five times.
- He led the AL in on-base percentage seven times.
- He won the AL MVP Award in 1911.
- He won the AL batting Triple Crown in 1909.
- He led the AL in batting average 12 times.

BARRY BONDS

Like many other great players, Barry Bonds starred at bat and with his glove. He was an excellent defender in the outfield. He hit for a high average and drew walks at a record pace. And he may have been the most dangerous

Bonds averaged 25 home runs in seven seasons with the Pittsburgh Pirates. Then he joined the San Francisco Giants in 1993 and took his hitting to another level. He hit at least 33 home runs in each of his first 12 seasons in San Francisco. In 2001, he hit 73 homers. That's the most ever in a season. His 762 career home runs beat Hank Aaron's all-time record. Bonds and other players of his era may have used steroids to improve their performances. He says that he never knowingly took them. What's certain is that baseball had never seen a player perform like Bonds.

BARRY BONDS STATS

- He was voted to play in 14 All-Star Games.
- He won the NL MVP Award seven times.
- His 2,558 career walks are the most in baseball history.
- He won the Silver Slugger award 12 times.
- He led the NL in on-base percentage 10 times.

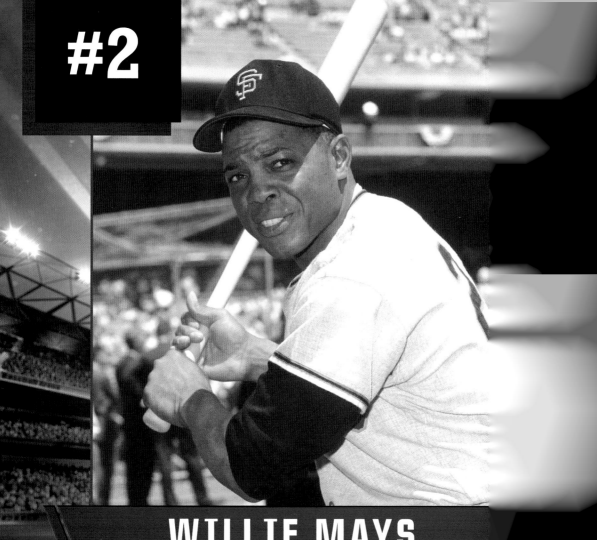

WILLIE MAYS

No player ever combined hitting and fielding better than Willie Mays. He began his pro career in the Negro Leagues at the age of 16. Four years later, he joined the New York Giants and won the Rookie of the Year Award. He spent most of the 1952 and 1953 seasons in the US Army. Then he returned to MLB in 1954 and helped the Giants win the World Series. His over-the-shoulder catch in Game 1 of the

series is one of the most famous plays in baseball history.

Mays caught more than 7,000 balls in the outfield during his career. Some were easy. Many he had to sprint to catch. Others he had to dive or leap for, robbing batters of hits and bringing the crowd to its feet. He hit singles and home runs. He stole bases and drew walks.

And he did it all with a joy for the game that rubbed off on fans and teammates alike.

WILLIE MAYS STATS

- He was voted to play in 24 All-Star Games.
- He won the All-Star Game MVP Award in 1963 and 1968.
- He won 12 Gold Glove Awards.
- He won the NL MVP Award in 1954 and 1965.
- His 660 home runs were the second most of all time when he retired.

#1

BABE RUTH

Babe Ruth was ahead of his time. He starred as a pitcher with the Boston Red Sox from 1914 to 1919. He set a record by throwing almost 30 innings in the World Series without giving up a run. His 29 home runs in 1919 also set an MLB record. Then the Red Sox sold Ruth to the New York Yankees.

The Yankees saw that Ruth had more power in his bat than his arm. They moved him to the outfield where he became the most dominant player in baseball history. Ruth played during an era when home runs weren't common. He took it upon himself to change that. He broke his own home run record in 1920 and again in 1921. In 1927, he smashed 60 homers. That was more home runs than 12 other teams hit all year. He retired in 1935 with 714 home runs, a record that stood for almost 40 years.

BABE RUTH STATS

▶ He led the AL in home runs 12 times.

▶ He led the AL in on-base percentage 10 times.

▶ He led the AL in runs eight times.

▶ He was a member of seven World Series winners.

▶ He led the AL in walks 11 times.

YOUR G.O.A.T.

AFTER READING ABOUT SOME OF BASEBALL'S GREATEST PLAYERS, HAVE YOUR OPINIONS CHANGED? If so, you can make your own top 10 list! Start by reading about baseball players of the past and present. Look at the books and websites on page 31. Do you have friends or family members who like baseball? See what they think. Maybe your librarians or teachers can point you toward more information about baseball.

Make your personal top 10 list of baseball's greatest players. Ask a friend to make one too. Then see if you have the same players on your lists. Chances are you won't. Talk it over and try to convince your friend that your list is the **G.O.A.T.!** You can write lots of top 10 lists about baseball. Who are the greatest pitchers? Who hit the most exciting home runs? It's up to you!

BASEBALL FACTS

▶ MLB's first All-Star Game took place in 1933. It was designed to lure fans to baseball games during the Great Depression (1929–1942), a time when banks failed and many people lost their jobs.

▶ Pitcher Jim Abbott was born without a right hand. He threw the ball left-handed and then quickly put his glove on in case the batter hit the ball in his direction. On September 4, 1993, Abbott pitched for the New York Yankees against the Cleveland Indians. He threw nine innings without giving up a hit.

▶ Cal Ripken Jr. started at shortstop for the Baltimore Orioles on May 30, 1982. He didn't miss a game until September 20, 1998. That's 2,632 games in a row, the most in MLB history.

▶ The first World Series was in 1903. The New York Yankees have won the series 27 times. No other team has won it more than 11 times.

GLOSSARY

batting average: the rate of hits per time at bat

center field: the area in the middle of the outfield

earned run average (ERA): the rate of earned runs allowed per nine innings pitched

fastball: a pitch thrown as fast as possible

on-base percentage: the rate at which a player reaches base per plate appearance

rookie: a first-year player

runs batted in (RBI): a run driven in by a batter

Silver Slugger award: a yearly award given to the best offensive player at each position

steroid: a chemical compound that includes hormones to promote muscle growth

Triple Crown: a title given to a pitcher who leads the league in wins, strikeouts, and ERA. For batters, the stats are home runs, batting average, and RBIs.

walk: four pitches outside of the strike zone that allow the batter to take first base

FURTHER INFORMATION

MLB All-Star FanFest
https://www.mlb.com/all-star/fanfest

MLB.com/Kids
http://mlb.mlb.com/mlb/kids/index.jsp

Monson, James. *Behind the Scenes Baseball*. Minneapolis: Lerner Publications, 2020.

Savage, Jeff. *Baseball Super Stats*. Minneapolis: Lerner Publications, 2018.

Sports Illustrated Kids—Baseball
https://www.sikids.com/baseball

Williams, Doug. *Baseball Season Ticket: The Ultimate Fan Guide*. Mendota Heights, MN: Press Box Books, 2019.

INDEX

PHOTO ACKNOWLEDGMENTS

Image credits: Wikimedia Commons (public domain), p. 4; Library of Congress (LC-DIG-ppmsca-18584), p. 6; Afro American Newspapers/Gado/Getty Images, p. 7; John Cordes/Icon Sportswire/Getty Images, p. 8; Dan Sanger/Icon Sportswire/ Getty Images, p. 9 (top); Jayne Kamin-Oncea/Getty Images, p. 9 (bottom); Bettmann/Getty Images, pp. 10, 11 (top), 14, 17, 18, 19 (top), 20; Focus on Sport/ Getty Images, pp. 11 (bottom), 13; Linda Cataffo/New York Daily News Archive/ Getty Images, p. 12; The Granger Collection, New York, p. 15 (top); George Silk/ The LIFE Picture Collection/Getty Images, p. 15 (bottom); AP Photo, p. 16; Sporting News/Getty Images, p. 17 (top); Diamond Images/Getty Images, pp. 19 (bottom), 25 (top); Library of Congress (LC-DIG-npcc-11955), p. 21 (top); Jed Jacobsohn/ Getty Images, p. 22; John Capella/Sports Imagery/Getty Images, p. 23 (top); Ezra Shaw/Getty Images, p. 23 (bottom); Louis Requena/Major League Baseball/ Getty Images, p. 24; Ralph Morse/The LIFE Picture Collection/Getty Images, p. 25 (bottom); Mark Rucker/Transcendental Graphics/Getty Images, p. 26; George Rinhart/Corbis Historical/Getty Images, p. 27 (top); Paul Thompson/Wikimedia Commons (public domain), p. 27 (bottom); Dan Thornberg/EyeEm Premium/Getty Images, p. 28. Design elements: Eugene Onischenko/Shutterstock.com; Iscatel/ Shutterstock.com; conrado/Shutterstock.com; DinoZ/Shutterstock.com.

Cover: Mark Cunningham/Getty Images (Mike Trout); Blank Archives/Getty Images (Babe Ruth); Eugene Onischenko/Shutterstock.com (stadium background); Iscatel/ Shutterstock.com (design element).